Remember to annotate as you read.

Notes

The Legend of El Dorado

Spanish explorers of the New World found vast treasures and gold in Mexico and South America. In 1521, Hernán Cortés conquered the Aztec Empire. He and his conquistadors took thousands of pounds of gold, silver, and precious jewels. Then, in 1533, Francisco Pizarro conquered the Inca Empire in South America. Like Cortés, he took all their gold. Both explorers brought fortunes back to Spain.

Tales of gold to be found in the New World spread, and soon men seeking their fortune sailed forth. As men searched for gold, the myth of El Dorado, a city covered with gold, spread and grew, too. El Dorado in Spanish means "gilded one." A custom of the rulers of the Muisca people in what is now Colombia helped foster the myth. Muisca kings coated themselves with tree sap, and then covered themselves with gold dust. Afterwards the king jumped into a lake and came out "clean." Explorers believed that if a king could cover himself with gold, then there had to be a city of gold—and so they searched for El Dorado. But there was no city of gold; it was only a myth.

The legend of El Dorado has also inspired writers. Voltaire sets part of his classic novel Candide (1759) in El Dorado. Edgar Allan Poe's poem "Eldorado" (1849) tells of a knight searching for the famous city of gold. Poe's knight is on a quest, but will he find the city?

This Muisca figure on a golden raft is on display at the Gold Museum in Bogotá, Colombia.

Legendary Journeys

hmark
ATION

Legendary Journeys

Student Objectives

I will be able to:

- **Read and analyze literary texts related to the theme.**

- **Share ideas with my peers.**

- **Build my vocabulary knowledge.**

- **Practice research skills.**

Credits
Editor: Joanne Tangorra
Contributing Editors: Jeffrey B. Fuerst, Brett Kelly
Creative Director: Laurie Berger
Art Directors: Melody DeJesus, Kathryn DelVecchio-Kempa, Doug McGredy, Chris Moroch
Production: Kosta Triantafillis
Director of Photography: Doug Schneider
Photo Assistant: Jackie Friedman

Photo Credits: Table of Contents A, Page 9: The Lady of the Lake, illustration from 'King Arthur's Story', 1981 (colour litho), D'Achille, Gino (20th century) / Private Collection / Bridgeman Images; Table of Contents B, Page 12: © Moviestore collection Ltd / Alamy; Page 3A: © ClassicStock / Alamy; Page 4B: © Michael Freeman / Alamy; Page 5, Back Cover: Granger, NYC; Page 15: Courtesy of Veronica Martinez Medellin; Page 17: © Imaginechina/Corbis

Illustrations: Mike Love: pp. 22-27

Permissions: Excerpt from *Mulan Joins the Army* by Ouyang Yuqian, translated by Shiamin Kwa and Wilt L. Idema, Copyright © 2010 by Ouyang Yuqian. Reprinted by permission of Hackett Publishing Company, Inc. All rights reserved. Excerpt from *The Dark is Rising* by Susan Cooper reprinted with the permission of Margaret K. McElderry Books, an imprint of Simon & Schuster Children's Publishing Division. Text copyright © 1973 Susan Cooper; copyright renewed © 2001 Susan Cooper.

Printed in Dongguan, China. 8557/0819/16222

ISBN: 978-1-4900-9218-8

Tips for Text Annotation

As you read closely for different purposes, remember to annotate the text. Use the symbols below. Add new symbols in the spaces provided.

Symbol	Purpose
<u>underline</u>	Identify a key detail.
☆	Star an important idea in the margin.
① ② ③	Mark a sequence of events.
(magma)	Circle a key word or phrase.
?	Mark a question you have about information in the text. Write your question in the margin.
!	Indicate an idea in the text you find interesting. Comment on this idea in the margin.

Your annotations might look like this.

Notes

15   The accuracy of scanning potential dig sites also ① improved. In the 1950s, archaeologists first began using ☆ instruments called magnetometers to measure magnetic properties below the Earth's surface. Variations in magnetism in the soil, for example, can help identify the presence of objects (artifacts) or areas where human activities, such as cooking, occurred. ! <u>The results can be recorded and mapped to give an overview of a site for archaeological exploration.</u> ②

It's amazing what we can learn through technology!

16   Then, in the 1960s, lidar (light detection and ranging), which uses a combination of light pulses and radar, was attached to airplanes and used to scan for ? possible (excavation) sites. Later, in the 1970s, ground- ③ penetrating radar was used to identify structures buried beneath the ground.

How low do these planes fly?

LEXILE® is a trademark of MetaMetrics, Inc., and is registered in the United States and abroad.

E-book and digital teacher's guide available at benchmarkuniverse.com.

BENCHMARK EDUCATION COMPANY
145 Huguenot Street • New Rochelle, NY • 10801

Toll-Free 1-877-236-2465
www.benchmarkeducation.com
www.benchmarkuniverse.com

Table of Contents

Essential Question

What inspires a quest?

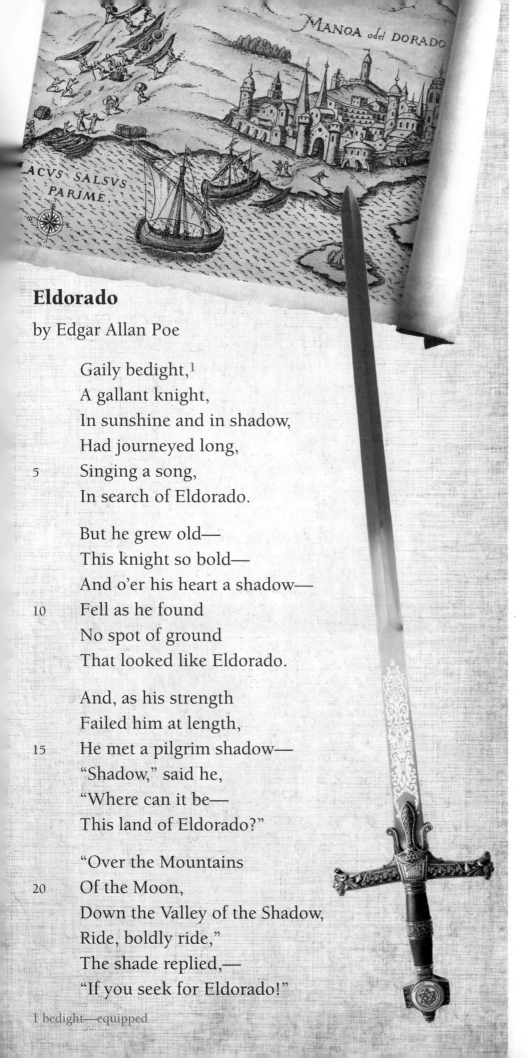

Eldorado

by Edgar Allan Poe

> Gaily bedight,[1]
> A gallant knight,
> In sunshine and in shadow,
> Had journeyed long,
> 5 Singing a song,
> In search of Eldorado.
>
> But he grew old—
> This knight so bold—
> And o'er his heart a shadow—
> 10 Fell as he found
> No spot of ground
> That looked like Eldorado.
>
> And, as his strength
> Failed him at length,
> 15 He met a pilgrim shadow—
> "Shadow," said he,
> "Where can it be—
> This land of Eldorado?"
>
> "Over the Mountains
> 20 Of the Moon,
> Down the Valley of the Shadow,
> Ride, boldly ride,"
> The shade replied,—
> "If you seek for Eldorado!"

1 bedight—equipped

Remember to annotate as you read.

The Legend of King Arthur

King Arthur was a legendary ruler of England in the sixth century. According to some legends, only Arthur was able to pull a sword from a stone, thus proving he was heir to the throne. With his Knights of the Round Table, Arthur embarked on numerous quests and adventures, righting wrongs and defending the kingdom. Arthur and his knights killed dragons, rescued damsels in distress, and fought bravely. Arthur was a good and just king, proud but also filled with compassion. He and his knights followed a strict code of chivalry; they acted with honor and integrity. Camelot, the castle and court where King Arthur ruled, has become a symbol of a fair and just place. King Arthur's main adviser was Merlin, a wizard who could "know" the future, and so he often made sure that King Arthur lived and won his battles.

Historical records indicate that Arthur may have been based on a real person who lived in the late fifth and early sixth centuries. Over time, as the tales were retold, his deeds and successes grew in importance, and led to the telling of new tales. Thus, a legend was born.

Howard Pyle's illustration (1903) of King Arthur

Renowned nineteenth-century French artist Gustave Doré created this engraving for Alfred Tennyson's *Idylls of the King*, 1868. The illustration depicts Merlin advising King Arthur.

Notes

King Arthur and his Knights of the Round Table have appeared in plays, poems, and books. Noted nineteenth-century British poet Alfred Tennyson wrote "Idylls of the King," a long, narrative poem that tells the saga of King Arthur. Arthurian legend has been the subject of a long-running Broadway musical, Camelot, *as well as feature films and television series. Arthur, his knights, and their exploits have directly influenced dozens of writers and modern works of literature by serving as the template for noble-minded heroic quests.*

The story on the following pages is from a collection of Arthurian tales called King Arthur: Tales of the Round Table, *originally published in 1902. At this point early in the story, Merlin has rescued Arthur from a battle and helped to heal him.*

The Sword Excalibur

an excerpt from
King Arthur: Tales of the Round Table

by Andrew Lang

1   King Arthur had fought a hard battle with the tallest knight in all the land. And though he struck hard and well, he would have been slain had not Merlin enchanted the knight. Merlin cast him into a deep sleep. Then he brought the king to a hermit who had studied the art of healing. The hermit cured all his wounds in three days. Then Arthur and Merlin waited no longer, but gave the hermit thanks and departed.

2   As they rode together Arthur said, "I have no sword," but Merlin bade him be patient and told him he would soon give him one. In a little while, they came to a large lake. Arthur beheld an arm rising out of the water in the midst of the lake and holding up a sword.

3   "Look!" said Merlin, "that is the sword I spoke of." And the king looked again, and a maiden stood upon the water. "That is the Lady of the Lake," said Merlin, "and she is coming to you. If you ask her courteously, she will give you the sword."

4   So when the maiden drew near, Arthur saluted her and said, "Maiden, I pray you tell me whose sword is that which an arm is holding out of the water? I wish it were mine, for I have lost my sword."

5   "That sword is mine, King Arthur," answered she, "and I will give it to you, if you in return will give me a gift when I ask you."

6   "By my faith," said the king, "I will give you whatever gift you ask."

7   "Well," said the maiden, "get into the barge yonder. Row yourself to the sword, and take it and the scabbard with you." For this was the sword Excalibur. "As for *my* gift, I will ask it in my own time."

8   Then King Arthur and Merlin dismounted from their horses and tied them up safely. They went into the barge, and when they came to the place where the arm was holding the sword, Arthur took it by the handle. The arm disappeared.

9   And they brought the sword back to land. As they rode, the king looked lovingly on his sword. Merlin saw, and smiling, said, "Which do you like best, the sword or the scabbard?"

10   "I like the sword," answered Arthur.

11   "You are not wise to say that," replied Merlin, "for the scabbard is worth ten of the sword. And as long as it is buckled on you, you will lose no blood, however sorely you may be wounded."

12   So they rode into the town of Carlion. There, Arthur's knights gave them a glad welcome. They said that it was a joy to serve under a king who risked his life as much as any common man.

The Lady of the Lake, 1981, by Gino D'Achille

Word Study Read

Remember to annotate as you read.

The Boy Who Wanted Gold

1   There once was a youth named Billie who had heard of a wise old woman who lived in the Appalachian Mountains. She knew where a pot of gold was buried, and if you could catch her, she'd have to tell you where it was.

2   "I'm going off to find that old woman," Billie announced to his mother one day.

3   "Who are you to take her hard-earned gold?" was his mother's response. "If you want gold, get a job and work for it."

4   However, Billie was determined. He searched and searched until he was exhausted, but finally he discovered the woman in a cozy little cave, spinning wool into yarn. Creeping close, he caught hold of her gnarled wrist and demanded to know where she'd hidden the pot of gold.

5   "I'll tell you," she promised, "if you help me find my ball of wool."

6   He agreed, but when he let her go, the old woman and her spinning wheel promptly disappeared.

7   Undaunted, Billie searched until he found her again, this time seated at a loom, weaving her yarn into a colorful design. The woman shook her head and scolded, "If you want gold so much, why don't you earn it?"

8   Billie ignored her question and refused to release her, until she pointed to an oak tree, saying, "That's where the gold is buried."

9   Billie hung his yellow knapsack on the oak to mark it and then hurried home for a shovel. When he returned, he found that the crafty old woman had outwitted him once again. Hanging from every single oak on the mountainside was a yellow knapsack. Chagrined, Billie realized it would be more trouble to dig under all those trees than to get a job, and so he decided to work for his gold after all.

BuildReflectWrite

Build Knowledge

In "Eldorado" by Edgar Allan Poe, what do you think is the author's purpose in repeating the word "shadow" in the poem? Describe how his use of the word changes as the poem develops.

Shadow in "Eldorado"	
First mention (line ___)	**Second mention (line ___)**
Third mention (line ___)	**Fourth mention (line ___)**
Author's purpose:	

Reflect

What inspires a quest?

Based on this week's texts, write down new ideas and questions you have about the essential question.

_____

_____

_____

_____

Building Research Skills

Narrative

Imagine that you have been asked to write a new version of a King Arthur legend. One of your guiding research questions is: What was the strict code of chivalry that knights in the Middle Ages had to follow? Read and take notes from two or more sources to answer the question. List your sources.

Remember to annotate as you read.

Notes

The Legend of Mulan

One of the most famous Chinese heroines, Hua Mulan is a symbol of loyalty and family devotion. Both qualities are greatly admired in the Chinese culture. The tale of a young woman who disguises herself as a man and joins the army to keep her aging father, a retired general, out of combat is one of China's most enduring stories. The subject of poems and plays, Mulan is often included in Chinese textbooks as well. An animated Disney movie from 1998 helped popularize the story in the United States.

As with King Arthur, historians debate whether Mulan was a real person, though some believe she probably lived during the Northern Wei dynasty (386–534 CE). The first known written account of Mulan is a ballad from the sixth century. An expanded and enhanced version of the poem appeared hundreds of years later during the Ming dynasty. From that version the legend of Mulan grew, and like the legend of King Arthur, took on new dimensions.

This scene is from *Mulan: Rise of a Warrior*, a 2009 Chinese film.

This stone statue of Mulan is in Singapore.

Whether Mulan was real or not, the story stems from historical truth. In the time that Mulan lived, the Chinese emperor forced one man from every family to join his army to protect against invaders. In the area of China where Mulan was from, it was not uncommon for people to be trained in martial arts, archery, and fencing. So, once outfitted in her father's old uniform, and with her hair shorn, Mulan could pass as a soldier. According to the story, Mulan remained a soldier for around twelve years until the army defeated the enemy and she returned home.

Mulan has become a role model for Chinese girls, who admire her courage and devotion to family. The story has considerable appeal in modern times because of its theme of gender equality.

On the following pages, read an English translation of the original poem. Then, to see how a story in one genre can be reinterpreted in another, read an English translation of a scene from a popular Chinese film from 1939.

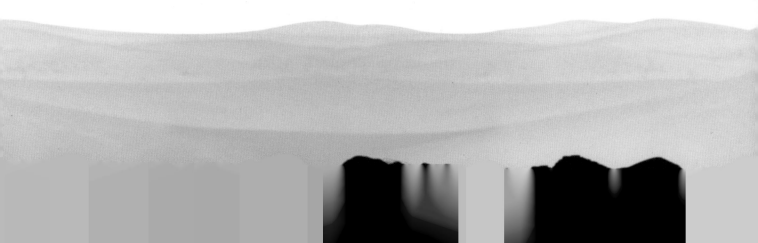

The Ballad of Mulan

"Say, maiden at your spinning wheel,
Why heave that deep-drawn sigh?
Is't fear, perchance, or love you feel?
Pray tell—oh, tell me why!"
5   "Nor fear nor love has moved my soul—
Away such idle thought!
A warrior's glory is the goal
By my ambition sought."
My father's cherished life to save,
10   My country to redeem,
The dangers of the field I'll brave:
I am not what I seem.
"No son has he his troop to lead,
No brother dear have I;
15   So I must mount my father's steed,
And to the battle hie."[1]
At dawn of day she quits her door,
At evening rests her head
Where loud the mountain torrents roar
20   And mail-clad soldiers tread.
The northern plains are gained at last,
The mountains sink from view;
The sun shines cold, and the wintry blast
It pierces through and through.
25   A thousand foes around her fall,
And red blood stains the ground;
But Mulan, who survives it all,
Returns with glory crowned.
Before the throne they bend the knee
30   In the palace of Chang'an,[2]

1 hie—go

2 Chang'an—the ancient capital of China, today known as Xi'an

Full many a knight of high degree,
But the bravest is Mulan.
"Nay, prince," she cries, "my duty's done,
No reward I desire;
35   But let me to my home begone,
To cheer my aged sire."
She nears the door of her father's home,
A chief with trumpet's blare;
But when she doffs her waving plume,
40   She stands a maiden fair.

Mulan Joins the Army

an excerpt from Act 1

by Ouyang Yuqian

The legend of Mulan was adapted into a play by the scholar Xu Wei in the sixteenth century. The Female Mulan Joins the Army in Place of Her Father *became well known and made Mulan a popular hero. Since then Mulan's story has been retold in poems, books, plays, operas, paintings, and movies. In this excerpt from the 1939 screenplay* Mulan Joins the Army, *Mulan has just returned home after hunting all day. Her parents scold her because they believe that it is not appropriate for girls to hunt.*

Father: These were all shot down by you?

Mulan: Of course they were all shot by me.

Father: I can't believe it.

Brother: I believe it. Sister is better at hunting than Daddy!

(*The elder sister quickly wags a finger at the boy and prevents him from saying more. MULAN gives SHULAN a loving look.*)

Father: In the future you can't go out anymore.

Mulan: All right.

Father: Hurry up and change your clothes.

Mulan: All right. (*She starts to walk away*)

Father: Come back. (*He addresses her as if giving orders*)

Father: I am punishing you with three days of weaving a
   bolt of silk. You can't come out until it is woven perfectly.
   (MULAN bows angelically) Understand?

Mulan: I understand, Daddy.

Father: *(hearing a sound)* Who's coming?

*(MULAN looks outside. An official MESSENGER has arrived,
delivering a document. MULAN'S FATHER greets him at the
door.)*

Messenger: Is this the home of the honorable Hua?

Father: Just lowly me.

Messenger: *(taking out the document)* So it is you. There is an
   official dispatch for you.

Father: Thank you, brother.

**This is a poster for a contemporary
Chinese movie about the legend of Mulan.**

(He takes the letter and, from his chest pocket, takes out some silver to give the happy messenger a tip. MULAN, delighted, takes aim with her bow and arrow and shoots the messenger's hat off, just as he receives the coin. He cowers in terror. We can hear her little brother laughing. MULAN'S FATHER picks up the hat and pulls out the arrow, and there are two small holes in the hat. The MESSENGER is very upset, and MULAN'S FATHER quickly pushes more coins into his hand.)

Father: Just a little something for you.

Messenger: *(weighing money in his hand, smiles again)* You are too kind. *(He examines his hat in wonder)* What a good marksman! Good-bye, good-bye!

(After he leaves, MULAN'S FATHER angrily rushes into the house, grasping the arrow. The family scurries away, and MULAN is the last to attempt to exit.)

Father: You little good for nothing . . .

Mulan: You didn't believe that I was a good shot, so I wanted to give you a little demonstration.

(FATHER moves to strike her with the arrow, and she runs out. Alone in the room, he looks at the arrow and smiles to himself, appreciatively. Then he looks at the envelope in his hand. On it is written "For the honorable Hua to break the seal.")

Father: Something definitely is . . . something definitely is happening on the borders, and I am needed again to join the army. *(He tears the letter open with the top of the arrow in his hand.)*

(Interior. MOTHER and FATHER are sitting alone together at the table in candlelight. FATHER is holding the envelope in his hand.)

Father: Joining the army this time, it's not certain that I will return alive. You have to take care of all matters of the household.

Mother: You are so old, and you haven't recovered fully from your illness. How can you bear the difficulties of the battleground?

(Cut to MULAN listening from her room, where she is weaving at the loom)

Mother: How can you tell me not to worry?

Father: *(sadly)* Our country takes care of the troops for a thousand days in exchange for calling on troops when it needs them. Now that the country is in trouble, every civilian must go to war.

(MULAN has stopped her weaving and is pressed up against the wall, listening intently)

Father: How could I live off the country's support and just stay at home? That wouldn't do. I am not concerned about myself, but I only worry that there is no one to take care of things if there are problems at home. If only Eldest Son had not died, things would be different. But we have two girls . . . *(camera pans over sleeping younger son)* and with Shulan still so young, how could he take my place to join the army to prevent this old man from dying in some other land?

(MULAN continues to eavesdrop)

Remember to annotate as you read.

A Civil War Soldier Named Hannah

1   Hannah chopped off her hair, pulled on a bulky jacket, and completed the transformation by rubbing dirt on her face. Now no one could discern she was really a young woman, off to volunteer in the War of Rebellion.

2   Hannah's family would've been shocked at her audacity, but she was determined to fight for the Union and for the end of slavery. The physical exam worried Hannah, but the harried physician simply checked that she had all her teeth and could hold a musket. She was in! After that, Hannah made sure to pitch her voice low and walk like a man. With her shorn hair, she looked enough like a teenage boy to fool the other soldiers.

3   Hannah took the name of Albert. It was spring, and rain had turned the roads and fields muddy. Hannah/Albert was shocked at the rampant illness in the army encampment; every day, soldiers died from diseases like influenza or dysentery, or infections from wounds that hadn't healed properly. Hannah also fell ill, but fortunately recovered.

4   The day was filled with drills, broken only by an occasional stint at guard duty—but at last the order came to march. A thunderstorm blew in, and Hannah had to battle both mud and tiredness as she and the other soldiers slogged toward their first fight.

5   That night, as her company made camp, tensions were high. Everyone knew that tomorrow would mark the commencement of the group's first battle. When, on the next day, the captain yelled, "Charge!" Hannah took a deep breath, raised her musket, and ran forward with the others.

6   Little did Hannah know that she was one of about 400 women who disguised themselves as men to fight on the Union or Confederate side in the Civil War.

BuildReflectWrite

Build Knowledge

Compare and contrast the story of Mulan as told in "The Ballad of Mulan" and "Mulan Joins the Army."

	"The Ballad of Mulan"	"Mulan Joins the Army"
Similarities		
Differences		
Decide which genre is more effective in telling the story of Mulan and explain why.		

Reflect

What inspires a quest?

Based on this week's texts, write down new ideas and questions you have about the essential question.

_____

_____

_____

_____

_____

Building Research Skills

Informative/Explanatory

Imagine that you have been asked to write a research paper about ancient China during the time of Mulan. One of your guiding research questions is: What was the Northern Wei dynasty? How long did it last? What was the culture? Read and take notes from two or more sources to answer the question. List your sources.

Remember to annotate as you read.

Midwinter Day

an excerpt from *The Dark Is Rising*

by Susan Cooper

The Dark Is Rising is *the second novel in an award-winning series of British fantasy adventures originally published between 1965 and 1977. On his eleventh birthday, Will Stanton discovers he is one of the Old Ones, magical immortals who work to keep the world safe from the evil, and equally powerful, Great Lords of the Dark. Will is on a quest to find six signs, medallions that can repel the dark forces. Like the knights in King Arthur tales, Will, a force for good, must battle the forces of evil (called Light and Dark in the novels). Throughout the series there are additional connections to King Arthur—from a search for the Holy Grail to characters similar to Merlin and the Lady of the Lake.*

In the excerpt that follows, Will has left his home and is questioned about being one of the Old Ones. He shows his medallion, which proves he is one of the Old Ones. Then the evil Rider appears and the two do battle.

1 Will walked a little way down the road, beneath its narrow roof of blue sky. He put a hand inside his jacket to touch the circle on his belt, and the iron was icy-cold. He was beginning to know what that meant by now. But there was no sign of the Rider;[1] he could not even see any tracks left by the black horse's feet. And he was not thinking of evil encounters. He could feel only that something was drawing him, more and more strongly, towards the place where in his own time Dawsons' Farm would stand.

2 He found the narrow side-lane and turned down it. The track went on a long way, winding in gentle turns. There seemed to be a lot of scrub in this part of the forest; the branching tops of small trees and bushes jutted snow-laden from the mounding drifts, like white anglers from white rounded heads. And then round the next bend, Will saw before him a low square hut with rough-daubed clay walls and a roof high with a hat of snow like a thick-iced cake. In the doorway, paused irresolute with one hand on the ricketty door, stood the shambling old tramp of the day before. The long grey hair was the same, and so were the clothes and the wizened, crafty face.

1 (Black) Rider—Will's nemesis, one of the Great Lords of the Dark

3   Will came close to the old man and said, as Farmer Dawson had said the day before: "So the Walker[2] is abroad."

4   "Only the one," said the old man. "Only me. And what's it to you?" He sniffed, squinting sideways at Will, and rubbed his nose on one greasy sleeve.

5   "I want you to tell me some things," Will said, more boldly than he felt. "I want to know why you were hanging around yesterday. Why you were watching. Why the rooks[3] came after you. I want to know," he said in a sudden honest rush, "what it means that you are the Walker."

6   At the mention of the rooks the old man had flinched closer to the hut, his eyes flickering nervously up at the treetops; but now he looked at Will in sharper suspicion than before. "You can't be the one!" he said.

7   "I can't be what?"

2 Walker—a human who betrayed the forces of good and was cursed to carry one of the six signs

3 rooks—a type of crow; in the book, they are servants of the Dark

8   "You can't be . . . you ought to know all this. Specially about those hellish birds. Trying to trick me, eh? Trying to trick a poor old man. You're out with the Rider, ain't you? You're his boy, ain't you, eh?"

9   "Of course not," Will said. "I don't know what you mean." He looked at the wretched hut; the lane ended here, but there was scarcely even a proper clearing. The trees stood close all round them, shutting out much of the sun. He said, suddenly desolate, "Where's the farm?"

10   "There isn't any farm," said the old tramp impatiently. "Not yet. You ought to know . . ." He sniffed again violently, and murmured to himself; then his eyes narrowed and he came close to Will, peering into his face and giving off a strong repellent smell of ancient sweat and unwashed skin. "But you might be the one, you might. If you're carrying the first sign that the Old One gave you. Have you got it there, then? Show us. Show the old Walker the sign."

11   Trying hard not to back away in disgust, Will fumbled with the buttons of his jacket. He knew what *the sign* must be. But as he pushed the sheepskin aside to show the circle looped on his belt, his hand brushed against the smooth iron[4] and felt it burning, biting with icy cold; at the same moment he saw the old man leap backwards, cringing, staring not at him but behind him, over his shoulder. Will swung round, and saw the cloaked Rider on his midnight horse.

12   "Well met," said the Rider softly.

13   The old man squealed like a frightened rabbit and turned and ran, blundering through the snowdrifts into the trees. Will stood where he was, looking at the Rider, his heart thumping so fiercely that it was hard to breathe.

14   "It was unwise to leave the road, Will Stanton," said the man in the cloak, and his eyes blazed like blue stars. The black horse edged forward, forward; Will shrank back against the side of the flimsy hut, staring into the eyes, and then with a great effort he made his slow arm pull aside his jacket so that the iron circle on his belt showed clear. He gripped the belt at its side; the coldness of the sign was so intense that he could feel the force from it, like the radiation of a fierce, burning heat. And the Rider paused, and his eyes flickered.

4 iron—one of the six signs, one that Will already has in his possession; the six signs are each made of a different material and represent a different element: wood, bronze, iron, water, fire, and stone

15   "So you have one of them already." He hunched his shoulders strangely, and the horse tossed its head; both seemed to be gaining strength, to be growing taller. "One will not help you, not alone, not yet," said the Rider, and he grew and grew, looming against the white world, while his stallion neighed triumphantly, rearing up, its forefeet lashing the air so that Will could only press himself helpless against the wall. Horse and rider towered over him like a dark cloud, blotting out both snow and sun.

16   And then dimly he heard new sounds, and the rearing black shapes seemed to fall to one side, swept away by a blazing golden light, brilliant with fierce patterns of white-hot circles, sun, stars—Will blinked, and saw suddenly that it was the white mare from the smithy, rearing over him in turn. He grabbed frantically at the waving mane, and just as before he found himself jerked up onto the broad back, bent low over the mare's neck, clutching for his life. The great white horse let out a shrieking cry and leapt for the track through the trees, passing the shapeless black cloud that hung motionless in the clearing like smoke; passing everything in a rising gallop, until they came at last to the road, Huntercombe Lane, the road through Hunter's Combe.[5]

5 Hunter's Combe—the fictional town where *The Dark Is Rising* takes place; it is in Buckinghamshire, a county in south-central England

17   The movement of the great horse changed to a slow-rising, powerful lope, and Will heard the beating of his own heart in his ears as the world flashed by in a white blur. Then all at once greyness came around them, and the sun was blacked out. The wind wrenched into Will's collar and sleeves and boot-tops, ripping at his hair. Great clouds rushed towards them out of the north, closing in, huge grey-black thunderheads; the sky rumbled and growled. One white-misted gap remained, with a faint hint of blue behind it still, but it too was closing, closing. The white horse leapt at it desperately. Over his shoulder Will saw swooping towards them a darker shape even than the giant clouds: the Rider, towering, immense, his eyes two dreadful points of blue-white fire. Lightning flashed, thunder split the sky, and the mare leapt at the crashing clouds as the last gap closed.

18   And they were safe.

Legend

Raven Brings the Daylight

1   Long ago, when the world was brand new, the Inuit lived in darkness year round in their Arctic homeland. They had never seen daylight, so when Raven first described this phenomenon, they listened in disbelief. "Impossible! Illogical! You must be misinformed!" they exclaimed.

2   However, the young people yearned to know if Raven's incredible stories were true, so they begged him to fly south and bring back the daylight.

3   Raven refused, stating, "I'm too old to undertake such an arduous task."

4   The young people pleaded until finally he agreed. Raven flew for days through the unending dark of the north, and at length crossed into the land of daylight and vivid colors; the land of cerulean skies, verdant grass, and bright flowers.

5   Although Raven was exhausted from his long flight, he persevered, peering into various lodges until he saw a container filled with glowing balls of daylight. *If I were invisible,* he thought, *I could steal one of those balls.*

6   An idea occurred to him. He whispered in the ear of a small boy, encouraging him to beg his mother for a ball. Raven's pleas proved irresistible. The boy cried for a ball and his mother obliged, tying a string around it and giving it to him to play with. When the child went outside, Raven snatched the string and headed north as swiftly as his wings could flap.

7   When Raven arrived, he dropped the ball of daylight on the ground where it shattered and rose into the heavens. The shadows disappeared, and the snow sparkled so brightly it hurt people's eyes. Unfortunately, the ball of daylight could only shine for six months before it had to be recharged, so in summer, the Inuit people enjoy daylight, but in winter their world is dark.

BuildReflectWrite

Build Knowledge

Determine the central idea of "Midwinter Day" and explain how images from the text help to develop this idea. Cite specific examples from the excerpt.

Central Idea	Images	Explanation

Reflect

What inspires a quest?

Based on this week's texts, write down new ideas and questions you have about the essential question.

_____

_____

_____

_____

_____

Building Research Skills

Argument

You have been asked to write an essay in which you argue if King Arthur was real or only a legend. One of your guiding research questions is: What evidence is there to support the idea that King Arthur was a real person? Read and take notes from two or more sources to answer the question. List your sources.

Support for Collaborative Conversation

Discussion Prompts

Express ideas or opinions . . .

When I read _____, it made me think that _____.

Based on the information in _____, my [opinion/idea] is _____.

As I [listened to/read/watched] _____, it occurred to me that _____.

It was important that _____.

Gain the floor . . .

I would like to add a comment. _____.

Excuse me for interrupting, but _____.

That made me think of _____.

Build on a peer's idea or opinion . . .

That's an interesting point. It makes me think _____.

If _____, then maybe _____.

[Name] said _____. That could mean that _____.

Express agreement with a peer's idea . . .

I agree that _____ because _____.

I also feel that _____ because _____.

[Name] made the comment that _____, and I think that is important because _____.

Respectfully express disagreement . . .

I understand your point of view that _____, but in my opinion _____ because _____.

That is an interesting idea, but did you consider the fact that _____?

I do not agree that _____. I think that _____ because _____.

Ask a clarifying question . . .

You said _____. Could you explain what you mean by that?

I don't understand how your evidence supports that inference. Can you say more?

I'm not sure I understand. Are you saying that _____?

Clarify for others . . .

When I said _____, what I meant was that _____.

I reached my conclusion because _____.

Group Roles

Discussion director:
Your role is to guide the group's discussion. Ask your peers to explain and support their responses.

Notetaker:
Your job is to record the group's ideas and importa[nt] points of discussion.

Summarizer:
You will write a short summary of the group's comments and conclusio[ns.] Check with the group that it accurately reflects their ideas.

Connector:
In this role, you will look for connections between the group's discussion and ideas you've talked about in class or events that have happened in the real worl[d.]

Presenter:
Your role is to provide an overview of the group's discussion to the class.

Timekeeper:
Your job is to track the time and keep your peers on task.

Making Meaning with Words

Word	My Definition	My Sentence
ambition (p. 14)		
cherished (p. 14)		
desolate (p. 25)		
exploits (p. 7)		
flimsy (p. 26)		
grasping (p. 18)		
hermit (p. 8)		
idle (p. 14)		
intense (p. 26)		
saga (p. 7)		

Build Knowledge Across 10 Topic Strands

Government and Citizenship
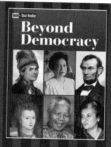
Beyond Democracy

Character

Characters at Crossroads

Life Science

Relationships in Nature

Point of View
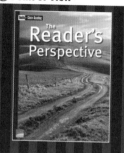
The Reader's Perspective

Technology and Society

Technology in the 21st Century

Theme

Legendary Journeys

History and Culture

Achievements of Ancient Cultures

Earth Science

Exploring Earth's Structures

Economics

Economic Expansion

Physical Science
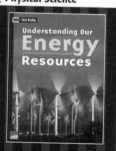
Understanding Our Energy Resources

Benchmark UNIVERSE.COM™
BENCHMARK EDUCATION COMPANY

Lexile 830L

Grade 6 • Unit 6
ISBN 978-1-4900-9218-

9 781490 092188